The Universe with Borscht

The Universe with Borscht

Poems by

Judith Sanders

© 2025 Judith Sanders. All rights reserved.
This material may not be reproduced in any form, published,
reprinted, recorded, performed, broadcast,
rewritten, or redistributed without
the explicit permission of Judith Sanders.
All such actions are strictly prohibited by law.

Cover image by freepik
Author photo by Daniel Lieberfeld

ISBN: 978-1-63980-985-1

Kelsay Books
502 South 1040 East, A-119
American Fork, Utah 84003
Kelsaybooks.com

Acknowledgments

Thanks to the publications in which versions of these poems first appeared.

Blue Heron Review: "Ferris Wheel"
A Critique of the Gods: "The Hearing"
Gyroscope Review: "Walking in the Cemetery during the Pandemic"
Ice Cream Poems (Concrete Wolf): "The Treat"
The Jewish Writing Project: "Bubbe and Zayde Take Me to the Ice Capades"
Keystone: Contemporary Poets on Pennsylvania (Penn State University Press): "Walking in the Cemetery during the Pandemic"
Light: "The Universe with Borscht"
Multiplicity: "All-Purpose Poem with Stain Remover"
Neologism: "Blue's Ballad"
Pittsburgh Post-Gazette: "The Treat"
Pittsburgh Quarterly: "A Moment"
Poemeleon: "Dishpan Meditations"
The Poet: "The Caribbean on a Shoestring"
Poetica: "*Yidische* Epithalamion"
Poets Speaking to Poets: Echoes and Tributes (ArsOmnia Press): "The Treat"
Red Wolf Journal: "Backwards, Before"
Relationships (Canadian Federation of Poets): "The Snow Leopard in the Teahouse"
Songs of Eretz Poetry Review: "Guide to My House"
Sugar Mule: "A Failure"

Contents

The Perfect Gift	13
You Want to Name It Like a Daughter	14
Bubbe and Zayde Take Me to the Ice Capades	16
A Tale of Two Haircuts	17
Ferris Wheel	19
The Treat	20
Yidische Epithalamion	22
This Qualified Applicant	25
Biker Chick, Ph.D.	27
Guide to My House	28
Dishpan Meditations	30
All-Purpose Poem with Stain Remover	35
A Moment	39
Stolen	41
Reading	44
Arithmetic	47
The Poetry Police	49
The Bad Companion	52
Lake of Sorrows	53
A Failure	56
Backwards, Before	58
The Hearing	60
The Universe with Borscht	62
Inventions	65
Walking in the Cemetery During the Pandemic	68
The Fall	70
Vaccination Odyssey	73
I Cook Dinner While Listening to the News	76
An Apple Has Many Uses	81
Piggy Bank	83
Slice of Life	85
My real name is	89

The Caribbean on a Shoestring	90
Roman Catechism	100
Blue's Ballad	106
Tough It Out, Babe	110
At Long Last (for now)	112
The Snow Leopard in the Teahouse	114

Notes

The Perfect Gift

Somewhere among the craft whiskeys, ceiling fans,
walruses sculpted from their own tusks,
Flexible Flyers, ten-speed blenders,
wind chimes, Adirondack chairs,
      is the object that expresses how much I

Among the diamond knife sharpeners, lace nightgowns,
orthotics, ergonomic can openers, magazine racks,
bullet-proof vests, leather steering wheel covers,
push-up bras, push mowers, crank ice-cream makers,
      there must be something that would

Among the tee shirts blazoned with sassy slogans,
tea lights molded into roses, lobsters, chili peppers,
shipped in containers hoisted by cranes,
unloaded at docks, stacked on shelves,
stamped with barcodes read by lasers

In the department stores, websites, souks,
farmers' markets, boutiques, crafts fairs,
among the glazed vases, carved birdhouses,
painted scarves, bulky sweaters, marbled soaps,
heirloom tomatoes, chunky salsas, artisanal cheeses

Out in the birdsong and feathered nests,
breezes ruffling pines and oaks shedding nuts,
shells and pebbles scattered along the shore,
colored fish darting through coral canyons,
glaciers calving, volcanoes smoking,
cosmic dust swirling, nuclear furnaces blasting stars,
      surely there is something

You Want to Name It Like a Daughter

You want to clasp that cloud
like the girl you never held

and caress the tresses of trees
like her hair,

stroke the sky's ether
like the milky silk of her cheek,

and fill your arms with meadows
cascading like her wedding dress.

You want to absorb its everyday words,
weed and blade, acorn and sparrow,

attentive as if to her baby babble,
her school stories, her staccato chatter,

and inhale the morning
like the fragrance of her scalp.

You want to dig a garden,
expel serpents, pull thistles,

as you would have built her swing set,
stocked her bookshelf, closet, lunchbox.

If floods drowned your flowers,
a slope slid, or the ground gaped,

if she had broken her leg or heart,
if such tragedies jumped your fences,

you would defend, prop and tend,
you would dig, replant, amend,

all to comfort, as with hugs and soups,
elixirs wrung from Time itself.

You know you can't fathom
the dialects of wind, bison, thunder,

and she too would have kept secrets,
slammed her door, hidden her journal.

You might not have understood
her music, clothing, choice of boyfriend.

She might have hissed *I hate you,*
as wildfires and hurricanes do.

Yet you wanted that tidal tug to her depths,
to have traced her tundra and forests,

as you want to plumb the ocean,
map the lands out every airplane window.

You don't know the names of the rivers
or clusters of lights below, but you yearn to,

as you yearn to know her name,
and how to let her, let all of it, go.

Bubbe and Zayde Take Me to the Ice Capades

On their Bronx subway platform,
they hold my hands.
She with her hatpin and cloth coat.
He in button-down and tie clip,
worn for this holiday
from cashiering at a newsstand.

We wait for the train to Manhattan,
where they never go, except today,
for me, their scrubbed, chubby grandchild,
who can't speak their language
and has her own room.

She was never yanked from school.
Would never know, God willing,
the soldiers, the nightmare of ripping
and smashing, the mother's screams.

My parents don't care about the Ice Capades,
the ladies in sequins, twirled by men in tights.
They are going to the symphony.

Bubbe and Zayde guard me, one on each side,
from the clatter of the oncoming train.
They do not ask why I wish to see
the Ice Capades, when my whole life
is a glide on ice, an escapade, a frolic.

A Tale of Two Haircuts

Once upon a time, I wanted
hair as long as Rapunzel's.

Hers unspooled in a golden ribbon,
strong enough to slide down.

Mine hung heavy, thick and brown,
only halfway to my waist.

The split ends were fascinating
when bored in the car or school,

but Mom decreed a trim.
I waited in the kitchen

while she quartered a chicken
with her black-handled shears.

She wiped off the guts and grease
and commanded me to turn around.

Snip, snip, the shears mocked,
as they furrowed my back.

Mom frowned. "It's crooked.
Have to straighten it out."

Snip, snip, in reverse.
"Just a little more."

The shears zigzagged up.
The clippings flurried down.

Mom swept them
into the dustpan.
•
These days I drive to a salon.
The hairdresser spins the chair

so I face my speckled old face,
staring from the mirror.

From a beaker of barbicide,
she extracts a comb.

She runs it through
my thinning gray bob

and asks
what I want.

Ferris Wheel

I danced past the hospital playroom
where bald children rode tricycles,
because you, my son, would get well.

You lay comatose on morphine
till at last a specialist
jumpstarted you.

Near home, from your car seat,
you spotted the annual carnival,
the whirling rides, the colored lights.

So I carried you, still limp,
in dinosaur pajamas, feverish head
tucked into the curve of my neck.

We threaded through
sturdy, scampering children
to the Ferris wheel.

Next year, I whispered
into the perfect shell of your ear,
we'll ride to the top,

and everything down here
will look small and far away.

The Treat

At the ice cream counter, the ample waitress
keeps scooping samples I don't want.

First a flavor called *White House,* "created
by the boss's granddad after a trip to DC
at cherry blossom time." No self-respecting
tree ever produced fruits like these red plastic
chews, here studding cotton balls soaked
in cold cough syrup. She chatters,
about a drunk who staggered in for a beer,
and her favorite *phosphate:* syrup, seltzer,
scoops of vanilla. I feel myself
getting fat. She offers yet another spoon:
an Alpine peak of *Blueberry Creme.* It tastes
like shaving lather. But she's friendly;
it's a Tuesday afternoon; a few stools over,
an elderly couple admire their twin
dripping sundaes. She strews rainbow
sprinkles for a prancing toddler,
even adorns the dish with a ribbon.
The bell over the door jingles; in strut
stubbled guys in overalls, catcalling
for triple dips of *White House.*

                                    Sheltered
by my shoulder, my slender son solemnly
celebrates turning thirteen-and-a-half
with what to him is the tallest, creamiest
of chocolate milkshakes, the kind that angels
must sip in heaven. One taste and I want
to rush to the dentist, but my son

can handle sweetness. So happy half-birthday,
son. You're halfway between so many
things. I count out bills, stack emptied
spoons. Soon you'll drink up the last drops
and leave, the bell jingling behind you.

Yidische Epithalamion

O! ye fair maidens
scattering rose petals,
singing odes to Hymen—
Ye can all just go home.

What? You didn't bring a coat?
In those gauzy togas,
you'll catch cold.

Take, take a few *regelach*
—the caterer, that *goniff,*
shouldn't get leftovers—
for your old *mammaleh*
waiting by the window.

Such *shayneh maidels*—
How her heart must break
every time she looks on you!

Must be a long bus ride
back to Olympus
so pish before you go.

(We got here a Ladies'
fancy-shmancy enough
for even a maiden's
pink *tuches.*)

Oy! fair *maidels,*
we don't need you.

We won't be twining ribbons
around maypoles
or wasting good rice
when in this sad world
children go hungry.

So rest for your next job,
maybe in that nice church
next door.

Here we eat and dance, yes,
before getting to business.

We know the others vow
to love and to cherish
till divorce do us part

but centuries of troubles
have sharpened our wits.

We know what we promise:

> *to wash and to dry*
> *to hammer and to nail*
> *to tear and to mend*
> *to joke and to weep*
> *to fight and make up*
> *to mourn and to dance*
> *to curse and to praise*
> *to work and to work*
> *and to work some more*
> *to fix the broken world*
> *that keeps on breaking*

then to retire to Florida.
And above all,

to tend the *goldeneh kinderleh*
who, from the muck
of our ancient suffering,
spring like shining miracles,

and let them go
to medical school or California
from where they never call
—those ingrates.

No, even today, we won't be
starry-eyed amid rose petals.

We'll stomp the glass
that held the sweet wine
and help each other
over the shards.

This Qualified Applicant

Can plié with graceful arm movements.
Can play a flute sonata (except the trills).
Once knew the main ideas
of several prominent philosophers.
Can produce a tasty, nutritious meal
of protein, starch, and vegetable
in under an hour. Usually.
Has mastered the difficult art
of shampooing a wiggly child.
Truly a master of complaining,
even under challenging conditions,
such as Caribbean vacations.
Can be jolly and spontaneous.
Known to dance around the house
lip-synching Janis Joplin into a spoon.
An absolute genius at wasting time
on non-lucrative pursuits, such as
curling ribbons and cultivating zinnias.
Knows what is wrong with the world
and can parse the sins in every newscast.
Can dream up utopias till cows come home.
Yet has portfolios of unsolvable dilemmas
requiring only a friend and a latté
for fullest exposition.
Although can hold still for years,
has traveled. Has sobbed into a kir
in Paris, in a delicious springtime.
Has tossed a Frisbee in the Sahara,
surely a unique accomplishment.
Have we discussed her capacity for guilt?
She is extremely responsible on that score.
An index of her self-recriminations

is available on request.
She can be very tidy, time permitting.
In fact, "She was tidy" will be carved
on her tombstone in neat letters.
That's just a joke, of course.
She is good at jokes
and would be a delight to run into
at the water cooler or photocopier.
We have not finished enumerating
her many talents. She can plunge
into oceans, even cold ones.
She can stargaze, rant, pun, kibbitz
(that dying art), window-shop, eavesdrop,
sunbathe, stare, and appreciate natural beauty.
But, we must admit, she overcooks lamb chops,
as her husband will tell you.
She is incapable of setting a mousetrap,
much less emptying one.
These are indeed deficiencies, but
with a little accommodation,
they need not affect her employability.
After all, she is dedicated
to making life pleasant for her associates.
She plumps pillows, never leaves milk out,
and always slices bagels before freezing.
In conclusion, given her qualifications
(and we have endeavored to present
as full a picture as we can),
we are certain she would be
an excellent employee,
if only the right position
could be found.

Biker Chick, Ph.D.

Roar down one-ways   blow by stop signs   trusty rusty ten-speed
  purebred racer   aerodynamic   lightning glider

I'm a cannonball   four-alarm demon   airborne dervish
  pedal-to-metal   toe-clipped mama   briefcase in bungees

Pummel headwinds   sail down straightaways   black-silk asphalt
  power-pump heart thumps   pant up back block   bull neck sweaty

Whoo-whee cresting   full-tilt downhill   whip past stuck bus
  flash of dahlias   bowl by ten-pin   leaden pedestrian

Glasses crooked   silk scarf flapping   skirt in clothespins
  stockings spattered   midlife butterfat   tickled by the breeze

Lean in low on   ram's-horn handlebars   bust the speed zone
  spew out crushed leaves   barrel by slowpokes   leashed to poodles

Cruise the complex   wham a trash can   clothesline gamut
  out-gun yap dog   duck to shortcut   give-the-slip alley

Twisting dodging   cracks curbs potholes   swerve a sand trap
  zip by trash truck   later alligator   can't catch me

Loop-de-loop wheelies   no-hands acrobat   blast past crosswalk
  skid to bike rack   rubber screeches   tornado of dust.

Clip on earrings   brush off blazer   hitch up half-slip
  pat down hairdo   heels click in hall   check office mail.

Count down the hours   till my next ride.

Guide to My House

My house is an unstarred attraction not to be missed.
It is a marvel of ordinary workmanship.
You may check your coat, if you can find a hanger.

Our tour begins underground in the vaults.
Here the Museum of Bygone Technologies
displays turntables, cassettes, and box TVs.
Archived in cardboard chests are artworks
created by the family heir in his youth
and the sacred remains of my dissertation.

Let us ascend to scullery, recently re-opened
since the sink was cleared of crockery.
Here the lady of the house—that would be me—
prepares feasts with her own soft hands.
The remains of one such repast,
a creamy paste of legume spread upon
a wheaten loaf, lie extant upon the counter.
Note the glassware of rich Ikean design.

The salon is a highlight of our tour.
The furnishings date from diverse periods:
Yard Sale, Grad Student, and Thrift Shoppe.
Observe the antique futon, certified
as The World's Most Uncomfortable Couch.
It can be opened for visiting dignitaries
only by mechanical engineers.

Next we mount the grand staircase
to the royal family's private apartments.
Here is the lord and lady's bedchamber,
strewn with garments and leathern footwear.
Family tradition forbids making the bed.
The historic humidifier gurgles, as it has
for centuries, like a dying fish.

Enjoy the view over the enclosed gardens
with their picturesque ruins of a swing-set.
The chain-link fence keeps out wild beasts,
such as rabbits and stray dogs.

The carriage house, alas, is closed to visitors,
lest they step on a rake or knock over a bicycle,
or disturb the delicate tapestries of spiderwebs.

Before you go, do enjoy a snack in the café.
Today's special is graham crackers
and a glass of water, much as the family
was known to consume in its heyday.

For a souvenir, consider a vintage dust bunny,
light, durable, and free for the sweeping
from under any bed.

Dishpan Meditations

Evening and everywhere,
at taps and tubs,
in streams and machines,
people are doing dishes.
•

Except the King. Haughty old stiff.
Surely he'd be nicer if he had to wash
his own Coronation goblet,
the Crown Prince's silver spoon,
or the tin bowl of the condemned man's
last meal.
•

Delicate probes into the stemware.
Muscular planing of the broiler pan.
Too bad there are no prizes
for virtuoso doing of the dishes.
•

My old aunt's engagement diamonds
hang loose around my finger.
They glint in the gray dishwater.

What if they whirl down the drain,
with the scraps and suds?
Tumble through the pipes
that spill into the sea?
Plummet through the deeps
until swallowed by a fish?

Lost forever—like my evening?
Which would I rather
magically recover?
•

Surely I was meant for greater things:
Not for scraping candle wax
or scrubbing greasy rings.
Not dishwater boiling hot
but wild nights on wings.

•

Bronx, 1965:
Mistress of the dishpan
as Shabbos candles gutter,
Bubbe in her hand-stitched apron
recounts her Yiddish tragedies
for my lipsticked mother
who contemplates her cigarette.
Awkward in my first girdle,
I dab a dishcloth at the china's
worn rosebuds.

Soon Bubbe will be done
with all those years of eating.
Spiders will crawl on the dishes,
interred in my mother's garage.

•

This dishwater has traveled the world.
Maybe it was an icicle in the Himalayas,
or a dolphin surfed its rainbow spray.
Maybe it rinsed a monk's rice bowl,
a hunter's knife, a princess's eggshell cup.

Let it run, jingling its braided silver
  over my rubber glove.
Let it run, trilling its wanderings,
  while I lean and listen,
tethered to the sink.
•

John Henry said to the dishwasher, *(unh)*
"A man ain't nothin' but a man." *(unh)*
He washed and he washed
till he broke his poor heart,
and he lay down his sponge
and he died, Oh Lord.
He lay down his sponge
and he died.
•

The bride in frothy white,
the groom in satin cummerbund,
after feeding each other cake,
should put on plastic aprons
and wash and dry the plate.
•

They'll be washin' in Boston,
Pittsburgh PA
Deep in the heart of Texas,
down in Frisco Bay
Shake that towel
Croon to that spoon
•

Doorbell. It's Sisyphus (again).
No need to shoulder a boulder
up some slippery slope.
The infernal eternal curse
reruns nightly at my dishpan.
Plus in here he can catch
Cassandra on NPR.

Hercules, though, won't show.
Claims he'd rather clean
even the Augean
stables, since he only
has to do that once.
•

Who scrubbed the hemlock
from Socrates' goblet?
Who rinsed Celia's kiss
from the cup?
Who swept the crumbs
from the Last Supper table?
Who will bleach the stains
from my favorite mug?
•

When my fingers stiffen with arthritis,
I'll recall this graveyard of burnt pots,
this junk heap of crusted crockery,
and envy my capacity
to engineer renewal.
•

Wash away today,
its husks and bones and skins,
its crumbs and crusts and rinds.

We've chewed up all its hours.
We've sucked out all its flavors,
down to the gristle and the grinds.

Cleanse the palate and the plate:
Down the drain go the dregs
of the day that we just ate.

•

As certain as death and taxes,
this daily praxis:
Doing dirty dishes.

All-Purpose Poem with Stain Remover

tried to write this all day

but this morning on the way to my desk I couldn't stand the specks on the bathroom mirror so went looking for the glass cleaner

thought okay first just empty that laundry basket sheets already folded just stick in closet no must stack neatly what if someone inspects

underneath some crumpled so stretch out on bed strip old sheets spray stains will get to desk soon

after dirty bedding to basement oops load wrinkling in dryer hang shirts lay rest flat

bathing suits sandy last week's vacation toss in gentle cycle still early haven't eaten

stuck in dream about old job where belong classroom or kitchen can't stop for existential whatever bowl of flakes cup of tea on porch in fresh air clear head bad news comics must keep informed

nesting doves have flown fun watching chicks fledge should mop droppings before afternoon rain neighbors' cats patrolled husband's allergic must wash hair off cushions which cycle delicate—low agitation sounds like personality type possibly mine

now son needs ride to internship registering voters hasn't finished bagel so ten minutes not enough for desk so sort laundry presoak washcloth mysterious goo he's ready roadwork takes forever chat election friends though he teenager still half asleep back quick mop porch does bleach harm tile should google once studied hermeneutics vs. semiotics now spatters vs. pellets which matters more deep thoughts interrupted husband reminds call bank check TOD mother's account lost in phone tree

lunch-time he wants to list Things to Do sure honey proofread his syllabus masons coming fix chimney need outside tap unscrew hose coil muddy where's old apron

mid-afternoon finally at desk upstairs forgot laptop downstairs took to café yesterday where air-conditioning doesn't smell like mold should clean unit unscrew tiny screws

back upstairs resist email but dental claim denied must contest prove am human spot motorcycles enter TIN lordy one acronym per day enough should schedule car maintenance overdue reset password link never comes.

So I take a nap. It's hot.

Eyes closed air-conditioned bedroom meditate om grateful house son husband mother joints mobile can still fold laundry

If lucky old decrepit someone else will not how I like

Am not in Syria Sudan not untouchable refugee forced to abandon desk sheets cushions porch

Am rich safe fed so is family more than millions billions including grandparents fled pogroms landed face-down in Depression

What find in self if called to fight fires survive famine eat bugs face torture resist Evil? As in closet order or mess?

Details lived to keep living ease others ensure son while registers voters has hat sunblock water though he teenager rolls eyes but what if sunburned dehydrated?

Do I envy Proust cork-lined room housekeeper to iron shirts bring brandy while he pens thousand pages uninterrupted? Rather be here down in the dirty?

Masons arrive climb ladders ferry mortar outside bedroom like window washers or Jacob's angels

Cut short nap carry out garbage last night's fish papers stinking up kitchen tie up tomatillo leggy fruits in funny paper lanterns should fertilize

While hunt for string recall how some paint Sistine Chapel discover penicillin receive Torah at Sinai leap out of gravity in ballet express Starry Night in whorls play Get Back on rooftop

While I unpin bathing suits from clothesline before rain still hope to get to desk before cook dinner salmon since hot how about cold yogurt-cuke-dill poach now so can chill

Tried to write this all day about mundane embedded in sublime and/or vice versa

Is life dance or slog on wire over abyss but with view?

No time to figure out caught in Brownian motion bumblebee jingle-jangle

When on deathbed will I wish sight of purple rainclouds massing had stopped me rinsing ants out of compost pail with insecticidal soap contributing to great cycle of creation destruction Larkin's million-petaled flower of being

A Moment

While chops sizzle and onions brown,
the radio intones failures, floods, and fires,
and the family cries its needs

Step out the kitchen door
Train your eyes on the clouds,
rumpled on the darkening sky

How big are they, you wonder,
and where are those cicadas with kazoos,
the bees that all day tilled the flowers?

How far is that brightest star
and why does it look like you could
cup it in your hand?

Would it sting like spattered fat?
Or hiss like a chip of ice
dissolving into vapor?

How old is the light filtering down,
and will you ever see another night?
Is anyone else out breathing the damp

drifting from the mountains?
Should you go, wander
to somewhere you can't imagine

A bar, a beach, a restaurant,
a grove of firs
haloed in moonlight?

The cicadas break off chirring
Crows caw a last goodnight
Bats swoop and disappear

Wipe your hands on your apron
How long have you stood here?
Go back inside

to anchor husband and children,
and turn down the flame
before dinner burns.

Stolen

Someone stole my silver twelve-speed
from a stairwell in 1979. The building
squatted on a dead-end street of cracked
sidewalks, crooked poles, a gas station.

I was pausing there after graduation,
on my way someplace better.
I glided out daily on my slim racer
to a job downtown and a future.

That bike was my only possession
that wasn't used, or jerry-rigged
out of cardboard and cinderblocks;
the rest fit in any borrowed car.

It spread its wings and we flew.
I took our strength for granted,
since my frame, like the bike's,
was forged of carbon steel.

We'd coasted back roads, looped
Lake Wyola rhymes-with-cola,
which I'd chant as we rolled,
for lack of much to think about.

It was terrible, being so young.
Nothing anchored me. I could've
drifted over that lake like mist,
not raising a ripple.

That morning I trotted downstairs
in my thrift-shop velvet skirt,
primed to pedal to work,
but my silver steed was gone.

I should've called the police,
dashed to the bus downtown,
but I pawed at mail slots,
peered under the doormat.

I checked parking meters,
darted into alleys spiked
with broken bottles, braved
the gas station dumpster.

I was young enough to call Mom.
"Don't mourn," she advised.
"Replace." And scratched up $300.
I pedaled a red ten-speed

for the next forty years,
sticking to main roads,
accumulating memories
and dents in my frame.

Now my gray bike has fat tires.
I don't love it, but I don't need to:
We have an EV and a furnished home
on a street shaded by mature trees.

If you see my silver twelve-speed,
please let me know. I hope it's not
rusting in some junkyard, rims bent,
spokes haywire, fork crumpled.

That a new owner keeps it oiled,
touched up with matching paint.
That it still leans into the wind,
gears shifting as smoothly

as wishing that everything
stolen could be replaced.

Reading

Sing in me, o Muse,
and everybody listen up:

Once upon a time,
on a dark and stormy night
and a bright May morning,
a page turned.

A knight rode into the forest.
A maiden swept the hearth.
A stranger arrived in the village.
An outcast desired the throne.
The daughters were penniless.
A man in a chair felt alone.

The plot thickened.
A conflict arose.
Symbols popped up:
Everything was something else.

On top of that, the narrator
had a point of view.
It was everywhere.
Could you trust it?

Characters developed.
They had strange names.
You could not remember
who was married to who.
Or whom. Whatever.

You are falling asleep.
The book is due back.

Where is a pencil?
You must remember that line.
How did the author do that?
That magic trick,
making words flare.

How many pages to go?
Where's a sportswear catalog?
Yet it is important to have read.
People will refer; you must
have something to say.

Someone is in trouble.
Please don't let it.
Now you can't put it down.
Can you believe this?
You want to wake everybody!
What a hero, what a schmuck,
how could she, it's unbelievable.
Yet you believe it.

You shuffle through the day,
while really you are
holding the hands of the dying,
sobbing at the graveside,
savoring the warmth
of that long-awaited kiss.

They lived happily ever after,
or died and were buried
under the back cover.

How long till you wonder,
Did I ever read that?

Arithmetic

Don't trust them.
They're squiggles in mud,
doodled with a stick.
Hatch-marks on scraps.
You could rub them out,
leaving a dirty shred.
A small black hole.

They're out to trick you.
Turn your back and they snigger
into their obtuse angles.
They slither out of reach
along their Mobius curves.
They babble in secret codes.
They slide off their graphs,
scatter and regroup.
They cavort behind x's and y's,
sticking out their tongues
to their square roots.

Can you hold one in your hand?
Can you eat it for breakfast?
Can you watch the sunset
with your arm over its shoulder?
What do they know about peaches,
babies, or lonesome clarinets?
About jumping in a freezing ocean
on a hot blue summer day?

Can they measure the distance
between you and me?
Can they weigh how much
you love me?
Can they locate
our common denominator?
Factor my anxiety?
Calculate how my education
compounds my interest?
Track my velocity
when I distrust you?
Explain how we are divided
although we have multiplied?

Now that you know:
Try to peel them off.
Look at your hand:
Try not to think of five.
Live the day
without chopping it
into the wedges
of the clock.
Resist the frenetic
slicing-and-dicing
by the second hand.
Beware stuffing the grid
on the wall calendar.

Recall that our ancestors
did not know they had two legs
or which child was first-born,
but they could not be conned
into counting their blessings.

The Poetry Police

The Poetry Police have a warrant for your arrest.
You are accused of fraud. Theft. Desecration.
    Forcing rhymes at gunpoint.
    Libeling parents and ex-lovers,
        assembling to testify against you.

The Poetry Police are banging on your garret door.
Quick—drafts under the bed, journals in the sink.
    Oh, hello, Officer, I was just watching reruns
        of Monday Night Football. Care to join me
            in a six-pack and pretzels?

The Poetry Police shove you up against the wall.
Soon you're shackled in the dock in an orange jumpsuit.
No more hipster black for you.
    You've sipped your last skinny *venti*.
    Nursed your last metrosexual appletini.
    Gyrated at your last *après*-conference dance.
Still, you might plead not guilty by reason of insanity
    or claim your writers' group led you astray.

The Judge is thin. She is famous. She is in a bad mood.
She just got off her hotline to Orpheus himself.
She dines with the editor of *The New Yorker*.
She rakes in scads from exposés of celebrity ex-husbands—
    Womanizing manic-depressive alcoholics,
        so handsome in tweeds and wild hair.
            They were some real poets.

She sizes you up over her designer frames.
She detects the foreign accent
        beneath your practiced vernacular.
She knows damn well you don't know
        a trochee from a trachea,
        a dactyl from a pterodactyl,
        a prolepsis from a prophylactic.

The Police display the evidence they've confiscated.
She deems your writing fit only for fortune cookies,
        calendars, cards, and teabags.
Need she remind you children are starving?
        That you are wasting her time.
        Your time. Your talents. If any.

Think of all the good you could be doing.
        The money you could be earning.
        The laundry you could be folding.
How happy your aged parents would be
        if you became a tax attorney
        or an orthodontist.
How will you explain to Saint Peter at the Pearly Gates
        why you diddled away your one precious life
            writing execrable verses nobody read?
You might as well just shoot pool.
        It would cost less in postage.
            You would have more friends.

Your punishment, she concludes, will be severe:
    The bailiff shall mimic your verses in silly accents.
    Inscribe you in the Registry of Crimes against Literature.
    Forbid you to set a metric foot
        within fifty yards of any School.
Your pages shall be clamped in public stocks.
First-readers and grad students will hurl critiques and tomatoes.
    They will deconstruct the remains
        before sauntering off, laughing,
            to sip wine at a book launch
                to which you are not invited.

Confess. Repent. Wring your handcuffed writing hand.
Swear on a stack of small-press journals you'll go straight:
    Write only grocery lists.
    Read only recipes.
    Limit *enjambment* to hopping on the bus.

Alas: No mercy. For you are a repeat offender.
Parole? Never—because you smirk at the pun.
    Don't give us that blank-verse stare.
    You know who you are.
The record—unpublished—speaks for itself.

This, for example.
In a tape loop implanted deep in your ear,
    the Judge decrees and decrees,
        This is not a poem.

The Bad Companion

I cooked for you.
You would not eat.

I took you shopping.
You would not choose.

I showed you autumn.
You would not marvel.

At the comedy,
your tears dripped.

When you slumped,
heads swung round.

All day you've muttered
while cracking your knuckles.

What can I give
if you always refuse?

What can I ask
if you never reply?

Stop squeezing my temples.
It is time to sleep.

With luck, we will have
many more years together.

Let us try
to make our peace.

Lake of Sorrows

Here is a lake I wept.
  It has evaporated,
leaving this bed of salt.

Here my baby broke.
Someone marked the spot
  with a cross. Perhaps
it was me. Shrouded
  with weeds, now dried,
that rustle like crepe
or the husk of a mobile
  twisting
over an empty crib.

Here my marriage
  foundered.
The rudder fell off
  and I drowned.
These barnacled ribs
  are all that remains.
Decaying
  on the lake bottom,
like an abandoned
  trap.

The cargo was a chest
  of coins. Scavengers
have had their way.
The lock lies rusting
  on a heap of pebbles.
The key
  was never found.

Here, half-buried,
　is the skeleton of youth.
The deformed limbs
　indicate blows
received when soft.
Who knows what shape
　it might have taken
when grown.

And here, the fossilized
　remains of old love.
Observe the archaic
　architecture of bones.
The shrunken wings
　that could never fly.
The feet too small
　to walk on.
The skull, an empty bowl,
　could not have contained
a brain capable
　of controlling a body
　of such size.

Over there I lowered
a diving bell
　down the trench
of memory
　where ancient creatures
drifted in starless dark.
The bends forced
　me to resurface.
The area remained
　uncharted.

Here, moisture still wells up.
The muck
　could suck us down.
So let's stay out
　on this platform
bolted into bedrock
　and shield our eyes
from the salt-crystals'
　glare.

A Failure

The sun fondled her face.
The earth massaged her feet.
The air ran its lips along her neck.

The sun offered entertainments:
It sparked diamonds from water.
Melted mists to unveil mountains.
Ignited silent fireworks
to oratorios by hidden birds.

The earth spread a feast:
Quinces and pineapples,
peaches and pistachios.
It spun trees into bouquets.
Embroidered hillsides
with Queen Anne's lace.

The air murmured distances,
rattling leaves like castanets.
It danced in fragrances
of pine and hazelnut,
lemon and wine.
It pressed upon her
the freshening rain.

She sent them all away.
Free of their fawning,
their opulent generosity
that demanded so much
gratitude. What a burden.
She would rather
sleep.

But even the dark said,
Let me love you.
Even the dark caressed her
with velvet hands.

Backwards, Before

That first evening we were
old. We remembered
too much. We knew
how vast the emptiness.
How crushing its granite
weight. So we wailed
through toothless
gums. Our little limbs
flapped.

By afternoon we began
to forget. The darkness
dropped from us. Our steps
lightened. Our hair
sprouted, curly
and lustrous. We noticed
orchids, potato chips, chocolate
kisses. The feathery
fingers of clouds tickled
our fancies. We could shake
our hips. We could slash
briars. We could light
fires.

By morning we lost
our way in the milky
light. Shapes loomed
and melted. We forgot
everything. Cobwebs
dangled and we
shuddered.

By dawn we lay
in ferns
in moonlight.
At last we understood
the empty language
of waves.
Birds sang *toura-loura*
and we
slept.

Back at twilight
everything glowed
blue. In dimming
mists, edges
blurred.

We could not tell
a firefly
from
a
star.

The Hearing

The bailiff summoned me from the stuffy waiting room.
A relief, getting off that hard folding chair.
Away from the others—snuffling, gassy, gossiping.

Inside, the gods slipped in and out of focus.
They were ranged behind a table,
but their heads kept changing shape.
Some had golden curls, yes.
Some wore woolly beards—probably false.
One leered under a witch hat, baring yellow fangs.
I thought I saw an eagle's beak, a cat's phosphorescent eye.

The wall clock's hands were spinning, and I had a lot on my mind.
How dare you keep me waiting, I plunged in, wagging a finger.
You know I'm busy wresting bread from the ground!
I'll get straight to the point: You are the sinners,
I accused, spittle already flying. Not us.
You make us love this beautiful world and then you snatch it away.
Your tortures are worse than the Inquisition's.
You lie about pits of serpents and lakes of scalding lead.
What's with the wine-water party tricks?
Why break laws that you yourself made?
I went right up to one and jabbed its sawdust chest.
Why boot us for eating the apple that you sweetened?
Where are all those vines and fig trees you promised?
Why not speak a language we can understand?
You'd be nowhere if we didn't believe in you.
From now on—I pounded the table—you're all out of a job!
No more building you fancy houses and roasting you savory meats.
No more sacrificing first fruits and—I punched the air—
No more first-borns!

But my shouts died away as if in a soundproof booth.
The gods had dozed off, their radiant heads drooping.
Time's up, the bailiff barked. Guards gripped my elbows.
Dissolve, vanish, go! I shouted, my feet back-pedaling.
You say you created us, but we created you.
I'm writing everything down, I insisted,
as we hurtled through the exit.
My book will be bigger than yours, *and you won't be in it!*

They shoved me in the elevator.
As each floor passed, a buzzer croaked.
From above I heard the bailiff cry, "Next!"

The Universe with Borscht

> "Better my borscht without the universe than the universe without my borscht."
> —Golde to her philosophizing husband at lunchtime,
> Sholem Aleichem, *Tevye the Dairyman*

I am,
so I think.

Rather,
I think,
so I am,
so I hear—

But instead
I think,
am I?

I feel like I am,
but I think
I might not
be.

Especially
before coffee.

I feel I'm so big
but know I'm so
otherwise.

I feel solid,
but my particles
are hollow.
When you call me airhead,
you're right.

How can life be so short
when one afternoon
pushing a stroller
lasts an eternity?

Yet 13.8 billion years
have passed in an eyeblink.

That's how long
my atoms have existed.
Which would explain why
my knees don't work.

If everything is made
of the same stardust,
why am I not as beautiful
as a slice of red onion?

The universe is expanding.
So is my waistline.

That black hole?
Maybe that's where
my car keys went.

Creatures
on the ocean's dark bottom
think that's all there is.
They're like me
without glasses.

There may be
worlds within worlds,
but is anything anywhere
as good as this cheesecake?

How can I think the crashing surf
represents eternity
when I know it looks different
to a mosquito or my dog?

I may be matter,
but I don't matter:
That's the matter.

I know everything
I know is wrong,
Yet I still believe it.

I eat breakfast
and go to work
as if the universe
depended on it.

Inventions

Aroma-gram
Charm your honey. Mail whiffs of salt air, roses, coffee.

Freeze-o-gram
Delight the grandkids with a scoop or a snowball.

Mini-Oceanarium
A vacation in a box. Relax as little waves roll onto its little beach.

Bloodhound App
Skunk or weed? Cologne or chemical? This Nose Knows.

Tollbooth Carwash
Drive-thru jets power off road salt and squished bugs.

Tollbooth Snack-o-rama
Preorder, then snatch that pizza as you whiz through.

Espresso à Go-Go
Solar-powered and portable. For the sophisticated *pique-nique*.

Urban Zipline
Why labor up when you can zip across?
Now with Spiderman Suction.

Bike-evator
No more huffing. Hook on and get towed. Every hill needs one.

Inflatable Bike Helmet
Packable protection. Rubber, not your head, meets the road.

Elephant Mask
Extend its flex straw. Sip safely even in crowded cafés.

Haircut Helmet
Auto-snips to your specs.
No more boring small talk with the hairdresser.

Prescription Windows
Check the weather without your glasses.

Window Star Chart
Built-in. Rotates with the seasons.
Never again mistake a satellite for Venus.

Home Wipers
Install on every window. Spritz, swipe, sparkle.

Le Plat-app-Plus
Identifies other diners' dishes that look so much better than yours.

Melonometer
Eliminates guesswork. Insert into rind. Pops up when ripe.

Roll-up Keyboard
Perfect for the pianist-on-the-move.

Heat the Beat
Solar guitar. Keeps fingers toasty while busking.
Bonus: Cordless amplification.

Solar Clothing
Warms the body instead of the house. So cozy on winter walks.

Solar Car Panel
Your vehicle's new roof. Charge as you drive.

Vacuum Slippers
Dust with sole.

Spousal Mood Tracker
Stay in synch with your mate.

Rooftops National Park
Greening the city's topmost layer.
Elevator up to meadows with views.

Snitty Epitaphs Catalog
"Skeptical—and right." And other nose-thumbs for the ages.

Athena's Wand
One wave and you are taller, smarter, younger, curlier.

Argument Detangler
Creme rinse for logic.

Defrictionator
Eases sticking points in relationships.

Hypothesis Generator
Possible answers to any question. Available in fact-free format.

Wonder Putty
All-purpose mending, from a cracked voice to a broken heart.

Everything Perfector
Soon to be released.

Walking in the Cemetery During the Pandemic

We're restless. We need
  to be walked.
The sidewalk is crowded,

but the cemetery lanes
  curve empty under the trees,
and the dead don't sneeze.

They socially distance,
  six feet under. Safer here
than among the living,

though strange to be living
  among the dead—
but we are always.

You'd expect stumps here,
  bare as skeletons,
the sky low and dark

as a coffin lid,
  leering vultures,
littered bones.

But it's Eden,
  the leaves fresh
and pretty as youth.

We note this one
  had a friend's name,
that one was young

or had my birth year.
  The implications
don't stick.

Mourners plant pinwheels,
  carve nicknames,
praise, and rhymes.

Some leave pebbles,
  as hard and enduring
as grief.

That weedy field
  will soon be
sown with coffins.

This cemetery could engulf
  the city, the dead
outnumbering the living.

While they decompose,
  under the blanket of grass,
we sniff lilacs they fertilize,

hum along with birdsong
  like odes, not dirges,
joke and hold hands.

Because for now,
  we can leave.

The Fall

November 2, 2020

On edge. On the edge. Might fall. This fall.
Mid-pandemic. Post-election. Climate teetering.

Gingkos flame like pyres. Maples glow acid red.
Their fever colors burned off summer's green.
We believed it would last, like all that
peace, health, and comfort we lived in.

We're cooped up, hemmed in, dodging strangers.
Can't lend a hand, even take mail from the carrier—
what else is he carrying?

Library's closed. My mask fogs my glasses.
Can't hug anyone but my husband.
Haven't put on earrings. Haven't gone anywhere
but upstairs, downstairs, around the block.
Confined as if old, ill, or guilty.

Squinting to see the world in my grain-of-sand
backyard. The neighbors' houses
seem sealed. We watch shrubs grow.
Time slows to stasis, smothered in amber.
Yet hurtling toward the fall.

Feel my hands: Colder than today's Arctic.
We sleep with jaws clenched. Wake ranting.
We're talk radios, spewing frustration.
No consolation that millions feel likewise.

We didn't want this. No one sick and dying.
No one desperate for rent. For a bag of food.
Working three jobs. Or none.
No one deported. After fleeing
hundreds of miles, with children.

No tattooed musclemen threatening with rifles.
No massacres in schools and synagogues.
No kneeling on necks. Only football fields.
No ice caps shrinking under skeletal polar bears.

Congregants beat their chests on Yom Kippur.
Moaning we have sinned. Have we? Most of us
are too small to dirty seas and skies.
To shave forests. To decimate tigers.
Not rich or loud enough to distort elections.

Hear o Israel: We are not One.
We are split, broken, shattered.
We all can't breathe.

Will my child curse me? All I invested
in constructing his happiness.
In a thirsty future, when thugs snatch
dignity at gunpoint, will creating him
seem selfish? Will he spare his offspring?

I want the real world, not a virtual one.
Warm people to talk and eat with,
without fearing that our breath is infected.
That we have poisoned the *neshama,*
the soul that God kissed into us.

This fall blaze will extinguish itself.
The fall will fall. Will we all fall down?
Ashes, ashes. Exiled, a snake's
oily temptations again our downfall.

Will we fall like Romans, once rulers
of the world, turned out among corpses
littering the roads, vultures circling?
Ahead, a thousand years of darkness.
A friend said, A thousand years?
I'd take it.

Vaccination Odyssey

When vaccines were scarce,
my husband heard of some
over in Ohio. We jumped
in the car and hustled west.

Trailer parks, gun shops, cows, mud.
Banners cursed from tumbledown barns:
"Trump No Bullshit" and "Fuck Biden."
Church signs preached in puns.

The hills flattened and woods yielded
to a grid of low-slung buildings
bordered with strips of mulch.
March sunlight hung watery-yellow.

Marquees praised fast foods.
Pick-ups glided over asphalt.
A breeze, clouds, a chorus
of disgruntled crows.

The drugstore doors parted.
The buffed floor wound through
a labyrinth of shelves layered
with deodorants, hair dye, pills.

I recalled how Athena had waved
her golden wand over Odysseus,
as he waited by the gate, as we did,
by the pharmacist's window.

Under a cloak of mist,
she rejuvenated the old warrior,
making him ruddy and tall,
mending his rags.

His hair curled like hyacinths,
red-gold on his burly shoulders.

Was the pharmacist our Athena,
the syringe her golden wand?

Would we too feel rejuvenated?
Beautified, fortified
for the overwhelming
joy of return?

After a siege in which we'd cowered
behind walls, masks, and screens;
shining Ilium was sacked;
heroes, breakers of horses, slain?

Later, Odysseus and Penelope
exchanged stories and embraces
on their deep-rooted bed.
Would we too recount our battles?

How we survived by our wits,
rowed against the current,
washed up on the rocks.
Wove and unwove shrouds.

We hoped we too would hug again.
Feast in our halls. Hand around wine
without contaminating the glass.
Stride our homeland, marveling.

Perhaps even feel inoculated
against cursing banners,
preachy puns, frictionless banalities,
chemicals camouflaged

as health aids. March dullness
before daffodils popped
from mulch, and greenery
clothed the parking-lot saplings.

Tennyson infers that after,
Odysseus felt bored.
His home island confined him.
Athena never visited again.

The mist evaporated.
My arm hurt. Back in the car
to traverse strange lands,
to our deep-rooted bed.

I Cook Dinner While Listening to the News

1.
The radio mutters,
Famine in Somalia.

I slit fat
girdling the lamb,
jab in slivered garlic.

*A mother carried her child
176 miles because
"We had nothing to eat."*

I scrub gold potatoes
and turn up the tap.

2.
In Ukraine, can't
boil a potato.

No heat.
No water.
No potato.

No husband
wanting dinner.

Empty plate.
Empty place.

3.
Torture in Iran.

I sauté scallops.
The fat spatters.

Splash cold water
on singed flesh.

4.
Dicing onions,
I tear up.

*Russia bombed
a maternity hospital.*

How endure
labor's agony
amid explosions?

I would press
my newborn's ear
tight to my heart,

so its drumroll alone
would welcome her.

5.
I mash avocadoes.
*Ukraine has lowered
the conscription age.*

If my son's life
were wasted
in a madman's war,

could I fire
at an enemy boy,
knowing his mother

was keeping
his dinner warm?

6.
Soup's boiling.
So is *the border crisis.*

I unbolt the door.
They rush in.

Mud on the carpet.
Strange smells.

They crowd
the guest room,
the den, my study.

They evolve
into Ismail, Omar,
Maria, José.

We send the children
chattering off to school.

The soup pot empties.
Again. Again.
And again.

7.
Wildfires destroyed
all the homes in Paradise.

In the dining room,
I adjust the air conditioning

and fill glasses with ice.

8.
We turn off the news
during dinner.

We watch videos of gorillas
munching wild fruits

and Otis singing
Shake it like a bowl of soup.

We savor branzino
in cilantro pesto,

ignoring that gorillas
are endangered

and Otis
is shaking it
with the angels.

An Apple Has Many Uses

Practice counting to one.
Place it inside yourself:
Become a container for an apple.
Visit the tree that birthed it.
Introduce it to its cousin, the crabapple.
Hide it where no one can find it:
Like in the washing machine.
Slip it into a mailbox and run.
Juggle it.
Study its reflection in the mirror.
Sing it a song it might like.
Give it a little kiss.
Lick it from its perky cowlick
to its dimpled bottom.
Weigh it.
Cinch its circumference
with a measuring tape.
Have it photographed
in a bowler and mustache.
It would look just like grandfather.
Paint it blue.
Wear it as an earring.
Place it atop a wedding cake.
Adorn it with diamonds.
Or rhinestones, according
to your budget.
Position it as a sundial.
Tell it tales of famous apples,
Eve to Beatles to Steve Jobs.
Wax it for a hood ornament.
Make it a mascot. Go, Apples!
Toss it: Keep your eye on the apple.

Hurl it into an ocean
and dive in after.
Race to the rescue.
Or you'll have nothing to do.
Without your apple.
Sue it. For withering.
For abandoning you.
Drop it from a hot air balloon.
Put it in your pipe and smoke it.
Chuck it in the fire.
It will blacken and hiss.
Pierce it with a needle.
Use it as a bottle stopper.
Wash it in the dishwasher.
Take it to bed. Snuggle
under the covers.
Sleep tight, sweet apple.
Copulate with it
and breed baby apples.
Knit them cute sweaters.
Caps with pompoms.
Write it an ode:
Oh thou loveliest of apples.
Place it on a pedestal.
Award it a ribbon.
It is a prize apple.

Piggy Bank

Hello, Sotheby's? Don't hang up.
I know your caller ID pegs me
as just another broke poet,
no trust-fund baby
with deep pockets to empty
and penthouse walls to fill.

But last night I discovered
that lump under the futon
wasn't an oversized pea,
but a piggy bank

containing a cool hundred million,
royalties from a bunch of haiku
—little things I knock off—
which had slipped my mind,
busy as it is with important matters
like tallying rejection letters
and avoiding death and laundry.

This windfall superseded
all my get-rich-quick schemes,
like writing a hit pop song
or inventing a robot mower.

So of course I plan
to feed the hungry
on my block and the next,
repair the cruddy sidewalks,
and train neighborhood youth
to install solar panels.

I'll have a wad left over,
so I'll knock on every door
and ask how I can be of service.
I'll purchase a prom dress here,
a laptop there, and a set of dentures.

I'll still have a few million,
so that's why I'm calling you.

I thought I'd buy myself a Rothko.
Something I've always wanted,
more than some boring yacht
with gold-plated toilets.

I'd like one of those big ones
that looks, you know, like God
shimmering in a window.

Just a little reminder
of the indifference
of the universe,
the terrifying,
awesome, burning
beauty of the void.

Do you have any lying around?

Wait, Mr. Sotheby, turns out
those weren't gold coins,
only slugs from some arcade
and a few tarnished pennies.

Slice of Life

The phone refuses to roam.
My thoughts won't stop.

I'm dreaming of a white Christmas
but it's so globally warm
that confused daffodils
have upped periscopes
around inflated elves.

The winter sky hangs
glum as depression.

Witchy trees model
for Addams cartoons.

I'm California Dreamin'
of affordable real estate.

The computer rejects my password.
The printer disobeys my command.
They snicker behind my back.

I've been on hold over an hour.
The tape loop spits inanities
that defile the cathedral of my attention.

Last night's movie was terrible.
That couple crunched popcorn
as loudly as gravel spat from tires.

I must return the electric blanket
despite the restocking fee. I dislike
sleeping under hot chicken wire.

A man who had raised chickens
and collected a library of poetry
learned, from inside the camp,
his chickens and books are rubble.

The woman in line for milk
clutches her baby as it claws
her dry breast. Meanwhile,

God plays tiddlywinks.
Zeus cruises for another mortal.
The clouds blush at naked dawn.

An overloaded boat capsizes.
A boy who learned English
from movies screams help
perfectly but drowns anyway.

My thumb hurts from arthritis
although I do PT religiously
—a lie that helps me feel
like a better person.

I plan a vacation to ruins.
The builders were in tune
with Nature and the cosmos.
Atop their astonishing pyramids,
they eviscerated captives.

Should chipotle or cilantro
flavor tonight's salmon?

I try not to explode with
happiness at my child's jokes.
He knows all the Presidents
and the World's Largest Lakes.

Another mother's son
was shot dead.
The cop was afraid
of the Twizzler in his fist.

Dog-walkers thread
the crooked trashcans.
Better bored than bombed.

On the dishwasher rack,
I work a jigsaw of glasses,
while DeFunkt exhorts me
to party hearty. Or hardy.
But I can't wait
to read Proust in bed.

When my husband rolls over,
he takes all the covers.

Flying telescopes witness
stars' explosions. Should I

bake pear-ginger torte
or chocolate cheesecake
for New Year's?

Does the moral arc
bend or break? Or just
wiggle?

I'd tug them back,
but I'd rather feel cold
than wake him.

I'd bet my bottom dollar
things can only get better.
Unless they get worse.

My real name is

She Who Stops for Sunsets
She Who Has Never Known Hunger
She Who Jumps when Called
She Who Is Amazed
She Who Can't Stand It
She Who Is in the Wrong Body
She Who Wears the Wrong Clothes
She Who Knows Nothing
She Who Can Spell Cantaloupe
She Who Pretends to Be Happy
She Who Judges while Smiling
She Who Wants Everything Perfect
She Who Can Fold Fitted Sheets
She Who Wastes Time
She Who Has Been Spared
She Who Longs to Be a Dolphin
She Who Is an Atheist Who Prays
She Who Thinks Dark Chocolate Justifies the Pain of Existence
She Who Never Ever Exaggerates
She Who Invents Constellations
She Who Belongs in Another Century
She Who Belongs in Another Country
She Who Hides Her Eyes
She Who Is Unfit for Battle
She Who Blesses Blooming Trees
She Who Loves Children and Dogs from Afar
She Who Wants Everything Simple
She Who Wants Everyone to Get Along
She Who Knows She Might Die Tomorrow
She Who Does Not Know She Might Die Today
She Who Has Many Names
She Who Does Not Know Her Name

The Caribbean on a Shoestring

I.
We step off the plane
into another world.

Back home, mid-winter,
we've been hibernating
in a frozen burrow.

So we blink and wince,
startled by this silken sunlight,
this air, warm as a kiss.

II.
In the terminal, dancers in perma-press
"native" dress rotate to canned folk tunes.
Free paper cups of rum promise paradise.

We shoulder our packs and split off
from tourists with matching luggage,
herded into hotel vans.

We line up for the jitney
among spattered workers,
indecipherably still.

It chugs under arching palms,
their fronds murmuring
over rosaries of coconuts.

The radio dreams of White Christmas
while I misname the tropical flowers,
boas of luscious magenta.

Town's a jumble,
shacks and high-rises,
overgrown rubble, a goat,
peels in the gutter.

Shutters clatter, laundry flaps,
market women squat, men idle,
ganja wafts, top-heavy trucks teeter.

Down muddy byways, glimpses
of an azure sea so dazzling
that I must live here forever

III.
What do you want to do
before we're old?

Walk the beach and gaze at the sky
Hold your hand and kiss you
Tend a garden and sing in the shower
Bear sturdy babies who ripen in the sun
Worship every dawn with a choir of birds

So shall we cash out our mutual fund
Rent a casita on a hillside
Live on tortillas and sweets from the market
Do the least possible in every holy day
Long minutes full of insect hum and sunlight
So we can hear time breathe

Or would we get bored

IV.
Shave at night in cold water
Wring the socks, clammy since morning
Ignore cigarette burns in the sheets

Count the midnight noises:
Gunned motors, insomniac roosters, straggling revelers,
the creaking useless fan, snores through the walls,
the world's loudest fly

The sky is never as blue as in the posters
The hotel never as charming as in the guidebook
The perfect beach is too windy, buggy, blazing

The local cuisine tastes of hunger
and local color is a euphemism

Fret till daybreak
just like back home

V.
In El King Seafood,
elbows stick to the plastic tablecloth
despite the laboring fans

White bread smeared with margarine
Clump of cabbage, thick pink dressing

Can you translate the specials?
Should we try the curried goat?

Rice and beans again
Fried plantains too

Big families at big tables
Women in tight bright dresses,
hennaed hair, hoop earrings

Men freshly barbered,
exuding competing colognes

We're in rumpled traveling clothes

Salty chicken breast with garlic
Chewy pork chop with onion

Couples flaunt frilly babies like trophies

Bottle of water
Bottle of beer
Local, not bad

Can you understand what they're saying?
Do you want flan again?

The waiter sets the check
without looking at us,
the rich gringos,
sunburned, bug-bitten, tongue-tied,
reading the coins

VI.
Nighttime stroll through the square
past the adobe church strung with lights

Broken street lamps, a dry fountain,
children on bicycles without parents,
a weaving drunk, hand-painted signs

El Exquisito Bakery—dusty cracker boxes
El Grande Fish Market—a leaky refrigerator
El Nacional Party—peeling promises
El Tipico Bar—an open shed

where men hoot over dominoes
and a woman with dyed red hair
shakes a tambourine at the dark

VII.
Hitch out to Blue Lagoon
Guidebook gives it five stars
Past shuttered barbecue shacks
resorts gated like prisons
Down that dirt path to a quiet pool

What a beautiful place to be alone . . .

From behind trees, teenage boys
sidle up, jostle each other
The boldest offers to show us around
He's shirtless in frayed cutoffs
with a glossy sculpted torso
from beefcake or a god
The others snort and elbow
No thanks—but he shows us anyway

    Here Brooke Shields washed her face for its beauty
    The waters are a fountain of youth
    Would you like to buy this lovely conch shell?
    I dive for it myself down fifteen feet
    and polish it for many days with sand
    The hurricane blew off my mother's tin roof
    She has thirteen children, she lost her job at the hotel
    I am opening this coconut for you—very refreshing
    Miss, do not scratch—the bites can get infected
    Sir, your kitchen door is open (if you know what I mean)

The trail fades into brush and sand
He surveys his companions lolling on the rocks
the luminous waters of tropical paradise
the palm-fringed golden beach

Miss, can you get me a job on a cruise ship?
I would like, he says, to get away from here

We fish out precious money
Our guide accepts and vanishes
Thumbing back, we spot him
lording it at a snack shack
with chips and a spliff

VIII.
Overnight bus-ride to the next attraction
Squashed by a snoring fat man
who spills over half my seat

Sunrise stop at a café with clogged toilet
Don't dare order the food for the flies
Locals stare; they think
this backwater's the world

Traveling is making it hard
to eat, sleep, and pee

Bus toils up the mountain
Rounds hairpins without guardrails

Look—jutting through the pelt
of jungle trees like a broken bone—
the chipped tip of a pyramid

Behind the bus windows
we fade into the sun's glare
while ghosts of the lowlands
hoist blocks of stone

IX.
On the white sand beach packed with pasty tourists
lounges a Rasta in mirror shades and dreadlocks
that hang like licorice twists to his rippled shoulders
his slim loins sheathed in skimpy silk trunks

He's encircled by giggling redheads
sunburned secretaries from overcast England
who have stripped off their sensible tweeds
down to bikinis teensier than underwear
Their jolly beers slosh in the mad midday sun

All night in Holiday House
a Jamaican berates his sobbing
Swedish wife. Over the partition
seeps their reggae, ganja, fury
Down the dark hallway
their toddler roams

barefoot in a sagging diaper
his pale brown skin crusted
with pink calamine
He pauses to whine
at their locked door

Up at the club, portly white men
swallow iced drinks served
by the sweating black waiter
silent in a strangulating bowtie
I caught him red-handed
dragging off a sack of my allspice
They'll steal anything
that's not bolted down

Along the ragged back beach
where tourists don't go
unfinished villas vandalized by vines
studded with staring lizards
belong to drug lords who've been caught
Boys kick broken glass with bare feet
Yah, I have a garden in the hills
but there is only one vegetable
that I grow

Snorkeling to the reef, I recognize them:
a danger I didn't know I knew
Barracudas, hanging in blue stillness
sinister as a spray of bullets
thuggish underjaws spiked with teeth
I splash to shore and the lifeguard
who barely turns down his reggae radio
They only bite whatever shines

X.
On that steep hillside by a tin-roofed shack
once painted pink, a child with a runny nose
lolls barefoot among pecking chickens
One hand is in her mouth; from the other
a stick dangles. Inside, a woman at a window
swipes a dishrag over a cracked plate
She glances up at a glinting jet
and wonders about New York and LA

While I, inside that jet, pause in forgetting
about her down there, and how I, lazing
by a dappled stream, trailing my toes,
watched her splayed feet tread the rocky path
as she balanced a sack on her head
a yawning toddler on her hip
a baby slung across her breast

Up here in the blue, skimming
toward somewhere I call home for now
I think as I flip through a flight magazine
how I could have been she
weighted in place every day of my life

Roman Catechism

Why would you want to live here,
in tangled alleys bumpy with cobbles,
grouted with stubs and shards?

In such buildings, gaudy and faded
like old courtesans, powdered with grime,
frescoes smudged like yesterday's makeup,
gussied with chipped garlands,
roofs bewigged in scraggly grass.

Where brazen gulls rip piled garbage
and flaunt their prizes.

Where graffiti curses from blank walls,
from embankments caging the useless river
that tantrums in the rain.

Where you can't fathom the staccato chatter,
the operatic flourishes, the twinned emphatics
of mouths and hands, the suspect invocations
of pigs and madonnas.

Where you can't decipher the hieroglyphs,
the chiseled Braille of friezes,
the comix scrolled on naves' high margins.

Where groomed men strut
trailing smoke and cologne.

Where young women wobble on stilettos,
and crones lug sacks heavy as pails of water.

Where people subsist on wine and coffee,
on dessert for breakfast, on sleep in daylight,
on cigarettes and fashion and bold good looks.

Where you'll never know what goes on
inside the courtyards, behind the shutters.

Where you tire of looking at rubble
and imagining palaces.

Where every church stoop has its beggar,
its leather-faced centenarian,
shaking a cap or cup,
wheezing sarcastic blessings
through a grille of broken teeth.

Where you dispense tokens to buy pardons
from the triple amputee dozing in the gutter,
barefoot children vending roses,
the migrant with the ocean
still churning in his eyes.

Or push past into the church's cavern
to stare at stolen bling, at stone bishops
knocked flat on their backsides.

Where saints' fingers shrivel in caskets,
paintings insist on grisly martyrdoms,
and candles plead with the enormous gloom.

Where priests perform their pageants
to empty houses.

Where all sins can be forgiven,
so go ahead.

Where the street is a gauntlet
of people wanting something from you.
Touts troll outside restaurants,
casting hellos like hooks.
Hawkers of toys and purses
tempt with *good price good price*.

Where tourists trudge behind standard bearers
on a *via dolorosa*.

Where magicians make your wallet
disappear.

Where refugees loiter in parks,
wash in fountains, urinate in bushes,
reminding you of everything
you don't want to know.

Where monsters, gods, and nymphs,
centaurs, cupids, and satyrs,
cavort in such profusion
that your dreams seem pedestrian,
your notions of decoration
as dull as a cardboard box.

Where vacationers delight
in fruit parfaits and rainbow pastas,
around ash-black Bruno Giordino,
immolated for truth-telling,

or snap selfies at the Coliseum,
where murder was entertainment,
although the emperor was bored.

Where history is so hard,
to tell it breaks your jaw.

Where parties spill from wine bars,
and youths whose night will last forever,
whose clothes are flat-out gorgeous,
balance long-stemmed glasses
on the roofs of tiny cars.

Where each of the rare children
sports a balloon and a pastry.
The little Highness jumps a puddle
and blows charming kisses
to *Nonna* and *Mamma*.

Where window displays remind you
your possessions are all tawdry,
your clothes are simply hopeless,
your shoes a national disgrace.

So, why would you want to live here,
with more funerals than birthdays,
more histories than tomorrows,
more strangers than citizens,

more statues than children,
more laws than police,
more mythologies than news?

Why here, in alleys that untangle,
develop names and patterns,
strewn with useless decorations—
jasmine looping a doorframe,
a terrace fringed with ferns,
lush as Moses' beard.

Where rooftops, ridged and rippled
with domes, spires, and towers,
form a jumbled jigsaw
backlit by the sky.

Where you buy *pizza bianca,*
a crust all hot and crispy
—O transubstantiation at the baker's—
it tastes like the body of god.

And a lick of *bacio* gelato
makes heaven seem redundant
and sex like too much work.

Where an old gent at the deli
bows you to the pesto,
and the clerk who rents the bikes
is as handsome as a star.

Why do you want to live here,
in this place that draws you
from your own preoccupations
through its mazes to its vistas,

knowing you can never
know all about them all
or rise to each occasion
with the necessary awe?

In this place imbued with heartbreak,
because for reasons you can't remember,
or make no sense at all,

you must go elsewhere someday,
although you will be longing
like Odysseus for his homeland
for this confusion you once cherished

and you know life will never
be this complex and compelling
wherever else you live or travel,
never anywhere again.

Where you inserted a coin
to light a masterpiece
of sacred art.

Blue's Ballad

Blue had a head for constellations and a trusty supple grin
Bones slung to fly like arrows and a dimple in his chin
Palms crossed with lines like roadmaps and photographic eyes
Blank pages in his passport and a fistful of supplies

His father ate martinis, his mother nursed a trance
If they'd hushed the music, he'd have tried the dance
When old friends had all tied their knots to college pedigrees
He chose to sleep in hotels where he checked the sheets for fleas

No one could take him to the airport, so it was time to go
The roads spelled out black calligraphs on fields of snow below
He heard good news as rivers rushed full-throated to the sea
He loosened up his seatbelt and toasted hope tax-free

In Africa, in Europe, on a golf course, up a hall
In subterranean storerooms, in fluorescent shopping malls
In moonlit ruined arches, crumbled canyons, on dirt floors
With one foot in a slipper and the other out the door

Peas from cans by campfires, drumbeats in the ground
Barefoot live religions, sundials left unwound
Black market deals in bathrooms, drunks with tales to sell
Kids who cried for candy—Blue got through it all so well

His head a bursting album, photos spilled onto the floor
He began to take siestas which he'd never done before
"Good-by" in every language, coins left unexchanged
Travel was expensive: he'd bankrupted his brain

The countries passed like hours, some were fat and some were lean
He forgot a hundred places that once he'd sworn he'd seen
With no tablet for his theories, no socket for his songs
His flashlight broke, the night went dark, he'd traveled much too long

He made love on a carpet, the weave wove in his head
(He thought that dreams bred better on a floor than on a bed)
She called him cream and topaz, she called him lemon tree
One hand on his breastbone, her bottom on his knee

Her father swilled rum punches, her mother watered plants
They'd ignored her music, so she'd flown to Paris, France
She talked in nylon stockings, then not a stitch at all
Blue's ribs were bars, a prison cell; he flung them to the wall

She said:
"With your skin as bright as glass and your mouth like ripened dates
Your bones slung like arrows and your eyes as blue as fates
Your breath of smoke and spices and your heart of unhulled seeds
Your passport stamped with promises and your unlocked chest of deeds

"With your head for constellations and your pockets crumbed with sin
Your worn expensive stockings and the dimple in your chin
Your palms like broken roadmaps and your wrists hung loose with grace
Your tale of worn geography and your fallen angel face"

Blue counted up his prospects, mended buttons and his ways
The walls were thin, the climate bad, but still he planned to stay
He put his hopes in envelopes and sent them out express
He shaved now every morning, he let himself confess

There were apples in the bowl and poppies in the grass
Two plates on the table, he'd arrived somewhere at last
His map split at the seams, his palm was in a glove
The air was bright and smoky, he could not breathe for love

His spring tide was rising, his moon was slick and full
The stars slid off a necklace into hunter, dog, and bull
The ocean was enormous, it spilled into his shoe—
She bought a box of candles and blew one out for Blue

His boots down in the basement, his guides on some back shelf
He kissed her on the navel, he could not help himself
She was restless during breakfast, she ate tapping her feet
He cut himself while shaving when she warned how fate can cheat

She said:
"I hate apples, I hate poppies, I'm allergic to the sea
You're rough, you're tough, and all that stuff, and not the one for
　me
I'm this and that and other, so I'm not the one for you . . ."
While rolling up her carpet, she said such things to Blue

Notebooks stuffed with secrets, pennies in a jar
A suitcase bursting at the straps which Blue put in the car

He took her to the airport in the evening's draining light
He wept into her handkerchief and far into the night
When herons fly they beautify, their awkward bones expand
He watched them through a window, flat-footed on the land

She'd called him cream and topaz, she'd called him lemon tree
Her breath lapping his earlobe, her groin hot on his knee
Her spun words trailed in cobwebs too thick to swab away
Now strangers made him offers; he heard each word they'd say

There'd been apples in the bowl and poppies in the grass
The stars had hung as clean as beads, his tide had turned at last
He heard that she was somewhere—someplace to forget
He oiled his boots and broke his lease and cashed in his regret

The bus was in the station, the driver at the gate
Blue, behind a winding line, grew calm as it grew late
His backpack had been stolen—it was too heavy anyway
He closed his eyes and didn't watch as roads bore him away

With feet so heavy with the mud of everywhere he'd been
With temples scarred with traces of misuses of his grin
With maps of blue-vein mazes showing just beneath his skin
With pairs of empty pockets to warm empty fingers in

Tough It Out, Babe

Some hours you have to slog through

Hoist yourself over their boulders push through their drifts one frozen paw in front of the other

Like when driving mile after mile after mile past Reptile Land the Little League Hall of Fame the World's Largest Ball of String so-called rest stops that push junk food on truckers mesmerized by pinball machines

You scan the flatline of horizon hoping against hope for a bakery a museum a fruit stand how about a yurt or a chocolate castle but all you get are billboards admonishing you to pray or call a lawyer

Sometimes you have to trudge the tundra of a Tuesday twilight when it's wintry mix nothing in the fridge but baking soda the toilet paper ran out your bra pinches

You have to gird your loins even if you don't know where they are or how to gird if you need a girdle or a girder

You must pretend to be patient even if you have no patience for pushing through the last lap up the last hill sun in your eyes socks soaked you have to pee right now or you'll explode

Some nights you have to endure till it's not 3 am anymore so you can haul yourself through coffee-commute-cubicle even though hours later it's still 3 am which should be blasted off the clock

Although you wish a black hole would roll by like some cosmic trash compactor to crush this afternoon when the devil ate your keys you missed the last bus you sat on your glasses you broke a plate shards spattered both girls got headlice the sponge smells the milk's spoiled you're on hold nothing but ear worms and static

And the baseball game drags on without any hits the music is too loud louts are spilling beer the sun pounds down but you paid the kids are scribbling on their scorecards pulling each other's hair

So you start dancing the beat pumps you up but around the fifth deafening chorus you think they shoot horses by the tenth you wander off who needs this swarm in the ladies' this commercial break these stale peanuts these over-priced lukewarm drinks

Sometimes you read and read but never get to the end of this standardized test this wash cycle this rectal exam this root canal this stranger's confession this heat wave this overnight flight this election cycle this childhood this same old marital kerfuffle

You have to tough it out

till you wake up later in history

to cotton sheets sunshine strawberry pancakes a funky beat a fat baby a funny dog a blooming tree an unexpected gift a shared belly laugh an embrace

when you'll want to hold it, hold it right here

At Long Last (for now)

Because I am ready after all that yes
that's what it took but nothing was wasted no
so now I know how it's done how it's won
now I can see what I see need what I need
mean what I mean am ready set to go to get
whatever I never no never before could
what everyone else took and took
for granted.

Now I can throw off crutches and canes
delays and excuses and so walk upright
even run on rough ground or smooth
high road or low even go on water yes
now I know how to float avoid sharks
kick their teeth.

So I can relax be kind yet yes tell the truth
now I know how and who I am and how
and who you are and what the world is.
I comprehend the beauty the terror
how cruel the human race how power mad
how fragile the body how short the life
how the worst really happens how the best
eludes us.

Why did I not how could I not before?
I believed in Santas in Cinderellas in
Beatles in sports teams in movies but
now I can weight-lift realities at least I
think so.

Now you can give me from the cornucopia
my hands are open so scoop it all up but
if despite everything you can give nothing
nothing is fine fine if the cornucopia holds
only breath only everyday sunshine
clouds too are magnificent because now
I can live on nothing rather more than that
on anything.

I feel sure that I could come go
talk of Michelangelo or whatever
find and merge yes freely with the one
who fits because even if I continue
to be ejected from well everything
every door shut every opportunity
snuffed my wishes pouf in a puff
of candle smoke

still I am strong at least just now
and that is accolades enough
is champagne is a gold statuette
is success.

The Snow Leopard in the Teahouse

Come to bed and I'll tell you a story

Stop firing emails and filing bills
Soak the pot, forget the trash
Turn down the heat, turn off the lights

Come to bed now, love, and I'll tell you
about a snow leopard, and no, we are not
too old. Curl against me, I'll rub your back
even though you drive too slow
and sneeze too loud and overcook the pasta

This snow leopard's name is Jason
He has powerful shoulders, good for pouncing,
and a long tail that he flicks expressively
I'll tell you how he pads around the Himalayas
even though you don't earn enough money
and can't read a map to save your life

The sheets are cold, so snuggle close
Jason in his plush fur never gets cold,
but when he does, he goes to the teahouse
He lounges by the fire, sips hot sugary tea,
and nibbles pastries. He trades news
with the other snow leopards

But there isn't any. No cubs upset in school
or governments committing injustices
or bounced checks or broken washing machines

So Jason the snow leopard plays solitaire
and glances at the picture window
with its view of snowy peaks
tinted lavender at twilight

He is getting sleepy there by the fire
He wishes he had a girlfriend to curl up with
Maybe Lorinda with her muscular haunches
who springs lightly onto the rocks
and looks so distinguished
silhouetted against the sky

Because what is love but a story
we tell ourselves
What is it but choosing
to be kind

Jason the snow leopard
brushes the crumbs from his whiskers
He rests his handsome head
on crossed paws, and wraps his tail
around his fluffy underbelly

His eyelids droop
as the fire dies
as the mountains fade

So good night, my dearest love
If I snore, give me a shove
Good night
Good night

Notes

The title "You Want to Name It like a Daughter" is from Robert Walicki's poem "Some Kind of Blue" in *Fountain* (Main Street Rag Publishing Company, 2019).

In "All-Purpose Poem with Stain Remover," the "million-petaled flower / Of being" is from Philip Larkin's poem "The Old Fools" in *High Windows* (Faber and Faber, 1974).

The epigraph for the poem "The Universe with Borscht" is from "Chava" in *Tevye the Dairyman* by Sholem Aleichem, translated by Hillel Halkin (Schocken Books, 1987).

Arlene Weiner suggested the title of this collection. Michael Simms published in *Vox Populi* the poems that formed the core of my previous book, *In Deep*. Carol Ober advised about cover design. Jennifer Freed, a colleague in the Yale Women Writers Group, recommended Kelsay Books. Karen Kelsay and staff provided this forum. My Writing Community, Patrice Alaquiva, M. C. Benner Dixon, and Ellen Wilson, offered companionship and insight. Sharon Fagan McDermott and Robert Walicki, my poetry family, inspired poems and were partners in meaningful readings.

Thanks to Linda Bamber, Sherrie Bergman, Susan Brison, Theresa Brown, Miriam Deriso, Sherri Hallgren, Cara W. F. Hyson, Nancy Israel, Sigrid King, Lawrence Lieberfeld, Ron Linden, Julia Lisella, Elizabeth Muther, Richard Nelson, Hal Ober, Debra Osinsky, Thomas Trezise, Mary Werowinsky, my Yale circle, and dear ones not named here, for their friendship and support of my work.

I dedicate this book with love and gratitude to my mother, Ruth Sanders; my son, Jesse Lieberfeld; my joyful friend Deborah Johnson, who had to leave too soon; and my husband, Daniel Lieberfeld, for whom nothing short of the whole universe would be the perfect gift.

About the Author

Judith Sanders' poetry collection *In Deep* was published by Kelsay Books in 2022. Her writing has appeared in journals such as *Pleiades, The American Scholar, Calyx, Jewish Fiction,* and *Modern Language Studies;* on websites including *Vox Populi, Humor Darling,* and *Full Grown People;* and in the *Pittsburgh Post-Gazette*. Her poems won the Wergle Flomp Humor and Hart Crane Memorial prizes. Her prose was nominated for a Pushcart Prize and selected as a *Longreads* "Top 5." She earned a B.A. in literature from Yale, an M.A. in creative writing from Boston University, and a Ph.D. in English from Tufts. She has taught English at universities and independent schools, and in France on a Fulbright Fellowship. She lives in Pittsburgh.

www.ingramcontent.com/pod-product-compliance
Lightning Source LLC
Chambersburg PA
CBHW072200160426
43197CB00012B/2459